SCIENTISTS in ACTION!

Archaeologists!

Astronauts!

Big-Animal Vets!

Biomedical Engineers!

Civil Engineers!

Climatologists!

Crime Scene Techs!

Cyber Spy Hunters!

Marine Biologists!

Robot Builders!

SCIENTISTS in ACTION!

Marine Biologists!

By K.C. Kelley

Mason Crest
450 Parkway Drive, Suite D
Broomall, PA 19008
www.masoncrest.com

Printed and bound in the United States of America.

Series ISBN: 978-1-4222-3416-7
Hardback ISBN: 978-1-4222-3425-9
EBook ISBN: 978-1-4222-8486-5

First printing
1 3 5 7 9 8 6 4 2

Produced by Shoreline Publishing Group LLC
Santa Barbara, California
Editorial Director: James Buckley Jr.
Designer: Tom Carling, Carling Design Inc.
Production: Sandy Gordon
www.shorelinepublishing.com
Cover image: Dreamstimes.com/Frhojdysz

Library of Congress Cataloging-in-Publication Data
Kelley, K. C., author.
　　　Marine biologists! / by K.C. Kelley.
　　　pages cm. -- (Scientists in action!)
　　　Audience: Ages 12+ Audience: Grades 7 to 8
Includes bibliographical references and index.
ISBN 978-1-4222-3425-9 (hardback) -- ISBN 978-1-4222-3416-7 (series) -- ISBN 978-1-4222-8486-5 (ebook) 1. Marine biology--Juvenile literature. 2. Marine biologists--Juvenile literature.
I. Title.
QH91.16.K45 2016
578.77--dc23
　　　　　　　　　　　　　　2015007862

Contents

Key Icons to Look For

Words to Understand: These words with their easy-to-understand definitions will increase the reader's understanding of the text, while building vocabulary skills.

Sidebars: This boxed material within the main text allows readers to build knowledge, gain insights, explore possibilities, and broaden their perspectives by weaving together additional information to provide realistic and holistic perspectives.

Research Projects: Readers are pointed toward areas of further inquiry connected to each chapter. Suggestions are provided for projects that encourage deeper research and analysis.

Text-Dependent Questions: These questions send the reader back to the text for more careful attention to the evidence presented here.

Series Glossary of Key Terms: This back-of-the-book glossary contains terminology used throughout this series. Words found here increase the reader's ability to read and comprehend higher-level books and articles in this field.

Action!

*W*hales can't call 911. The massive marine animals, some of the largest creatures ever to live on Earth, have had to deal with humans entering their world for centuries. For a long time, people hunted whales. In fact, some countries still allow limited hunting. For the most part, though, the world knows how special whales are and tries to protect them. When a whale is in trouble and people can help, the call goes out for…marine biologists.

In early spring 2014, a humpback whale (like the one at left) became tangled in the ropes connected to a heavy crab trap. A whale-watching boat packed with tourists saw the struggling animal near Monterey Bay in northern California. The people reported what they saw to local experts. The Whale Entanglement Team (WET) was called in. The group of daring scientists, divers, and boat pilots are like a strike team for whales in trouble. The team carefully approached the whale and attached a tracking device to its back.

WORDS TO UNDERSTAND

flukes   the wide, flat parts of a whale's tail

It could not, however, reach the ropes at that time due to darkness and heavy seas.

The next day, the team members piloted a small boat toward the whale and were able to reach out with a pole and slice the rope. They then managed to grab more than 250 feet (76 m) of the rope, making it slightly easier for the whale to swim.

That was all they could reach. The heavy crab trap still dangled like an anchor from the whale. With every stroke of its mighty tail, the rough rope cut into the animal's skin.

Over the next two-plus weeks, the whale was tracked as it swam slowly south toward the Santa Barbara Channel. Whale watching boats, government craft, and the satellites overhead all kept watch of the whale, a young adult about 25 feet (7.6 m) long.

Finally, they determined that the whale was in real trouble. Also, the seas in the channel were safer for the boats and the animal. With flat water and little wind, making the final part of the rescue would be safe for all . . . probably.

It was time to act.

Climbing aboard a large ship from the National Oceanic and Aeronautic Administration (NOAA), the government agency that cares for the sea, team members headed into the channel. Once they were near the whale, the WET team launched small boats that could approach it safely.

As the whale slowly swam through the calm seas, almost within sight of land, the boats puttered close behind. The scientists on the boat all were wearing life vests, wet suits, and helmets. The inflatable boat was sturdy, but it would not withstand an accidental swipe from the **flukes** of a huge whale.

The scientists tracked the whale throughout the morning, waiting for the right moment to try to slice away the last ropes and the heavy trap.

The whale came to the surface to breathe—this was the moment. The team drove the boat right up behind the whale. Looking into the clear water, they stuck out a long pole with a very sharp knife at one end. Careful not to cut the sensitive flesh, they found the right spot. With a twist of the blade, the rescue was complete. The ropes spun off, the trap fell away, and the whale was free!

"It was a phenomenal experience," said Keith Yipp, a WET team member and marine biologist at SeaWorld. "These animals would perish if we didn't intervene. It wasn't their fault."

The best news? More than three months later, a group of students were on a whale-watching boat in Monterey Bay. They were taking part

As the tangled whale surfaces to breathe (spout at right), the WET team zips close in an inflatable. The long pole has a sharp knife at the end to slice through the rope binding the whale.

A humpback whale rests for a moment in the ocean. The ability to help whales that have been injured by humans is a very satisfying part of the job of a marine biologist.

in a whale count and studying them as part of a summer internship at the nearby aquarium. Several students saw a whale with a damaged tail. Photos were taken and compared to those of the whale that had been freed from the ropes. They were a match.

"The last time I saw this whale is when we watched it swim free after disentangling it in May in the Santa Barbara Channel," said Peggy Stap, a member of WET. "To know it swam all the way from there back to Monterey Bay is so amazing. It was wonderful to see it free and healthy."

Turns out whales can call 911, even if they can't dial.

The Scientists and Their Science

1

More than 70 percent of the earth is covered by water. That water is the source of our life, of our rainwater, and of snowfall that melts. It brings warmth to shorelines, soaks up dangerous gases from the air…and, of course, it's great to swim in!

The oceans of the world are filled with an amazing variety of animals, from microscopic **plankton** to the largest animals ever to live on the planet. By studying the ocean and everything that lives in it, marine biologists are doing work that is vital to the health of our planet. To do that job, they don't sit in a lab or spend time in dusty libraries. To find out what they need to find out, they are out in the oceans of the world, diving, discovering, and learning.

WORDS TO UNDERSTAND

plankton   an aquatic form of plant life

What Is Marine Biology?

arine means having to do with the seas. Biology is the study of life. So marine biology is the study of life in the oceans. These scientists do study the animals of the sea, but they also study the world those animals live in. A branch of science called oceanography focuses on the water itself, but marine biologists have to make

At sea aboard a research ship, a scientist carefully examines samples of krill, a tiny fish that is an important food source for whales. Marine biologists often do their work aboard ships like this one.

Types of Marine Biologists

Here are some specialties within the larger field of marine biology.

Science	Study of . . .
Aquaculture	fishing and food fish
Cetology	whales
Environmental Marine Bio	ocean health for animals
Ichthyology	fish
Marine Mammalogy	marine mammals
Microbiology	microscopic animals

the ocean part of their work at all times. You can't study an animal if you don't understand its habitat.

People who want to become marine biologists study sciences of all kinds. In college, they can earn a degree in the field. However, many experts now say that learning almost any science can translate into studying marine animals. A scientist studying the effects of acid rain on sea life has to understand the chemistry of the acid as well as the biology of the animals it is affecting. Future marine biologists might also study chemistry, oceanography, physics, or earth science.

With a college degree in hand, most marine biologists go on to earn advanced degrees, such as a master's or Ph.D. With those degrees, they can work for universities, laboratories, and research institutes. Companies that work in the ocean hire marine biologists. For example, an oil company that wants to build a drilling rig will work with marine biologists to study the ocean life in the area. Many marine biologists work for the federal or state government. They help protect the marine animals by making sure that lawmakers have the latest information.

Zoos and marine parks also employ marine biologists. They work with the trainers and zookeepers to make sure the animals are healthy. They are consulted when the zoo wants to bring in a new marine animal to make sure its home is made properly.

At universities, the scientists teach classes, but also take on research projects. Carol Blanchette is a senior research biologist at the University of California at Santa Barbara (UCSB).

"The most exciting stuff I've done was looking at upwelling ecosystems," she said. "An upwell means when cold water rises from the depths as it nears a coastline." Dr. Blanchette studied how the cold water affected the animals that lived in those areas. She writes articles about her research so other scientists can build on what she learned in her experiments.

Though they live on land part of their lives, penguins can be studied by marine biologists. Any animal that spends some of its life in the sea is part of the world that those scientists observe.

A kelp forest teeming with marine life is a hands-on observatory for a marine biologist who is skilled at diving. Seeing the animals in their home environment is a perfect way to learn more about them.

Animals, Plants, and More

Most people think of dolphins or whales when they think of marine biology. However, nowhere else in the world is life more diverse than in the ocean. Biologists can choose from a huge number of types of animals to study. They can even specialize in sea plants, which are another form of life. Steven Manley is a biology professor at California State University at Long Beach, and he specializes in the study of kelp, an underwater plant. In 2012, he and his team found that radiation from the 2011 Japanese nuclear disaster had reached kelp forests off California. Stasia Ferbey is a clam expert for a scientific research company in Canada. She studies those squishy animals and tries to find new species. The world of marine biologists is as diverse as the creatures it studies.

Life in the Field

Because all of the animals that marine biologists study are in the ocean, that's where the scientists spend a lot of their time. Whether investigating animals that live in tide pools or diving tens of thousands of feet below the surface to find new fish, marine biologists cover the globe in their work. Life as a marine biologist is not for someone who wants to be indoors all day.

"When you're out in the field, it's kind of important to be somebody who enjoys being outside and isn't afraid of weather," said Blanchette. "There are challenges thrown your way on a daily basis. It doesn't matter how hot or cold or stormy it is, you have a job to get done so you have to do it. When you're doing this, there are no hours, there's no clocking in and out. People who like that spirit of adventure will really like this work."

As we'll see in the next chapter, marine biologists have plenty of high-tech gear to help them. They have to be ready to use it, however, and that means being open to learning new techniques and methods.

A Curious Scientist

Marine biologists not only have to learn new techniques, they have to love learning itself. Scientists have to understand that they don't know everything, and that their work is one of constant discovery.

"The first thing you should have is natural curiosity and be a person who has a desire to understand how things work and why they work that way," Blanchette said. "That applies to all aspects of science, of course, but in marine biology we're trying to see why certain animals live in certain parts of the ocean or how they deal with different forces in their worlds."

In order to learn more about how sea turtles move through the ocean, this scientist has captured a pair of the animals. They are given a drug to put them to sleep. Once tagged, they will be released.

Sometimes being a marine biologist means getting your hands really, really dirty. Aboard a bobbing research vessel, these scientists are digging into mud from the sea floor in search of creatures.

Blanchette loves that part of her job. Like other marine biologists, she revels in the idea that the next watery morning might turn up something that changes the world.

"It's the spirit of adventure and curiosity that keeps us going," she said. "I'm out there trying to figure out answers to puzzles. Every day, you put together another little piece. If you enjoy that sort of problem solving, this is for you. It's your job, but you'd probably do it even if you weren't getting paid."

That feeling is present throughout the world of marine biologists. They come to their jobs with natural curiosity and a desire to learn more about the world of marine creatures. They have to get wet, they might be cold, they might have to be on a boat for days . . . but they love every minute. The idea that something they find might someday help humans live in better harmony with sea animals keeps them going back to the sea, again and again.

 # Text-Dependent Questions

1. What related fields of study can future marine biologists explore?
2. Name two places that marine biologists might work.
3. What does Dr. Blanchette say all scientists need?

 # Research Project

Look at the list of specialties on page 15. Which sound most interesting to you? Do a little research to find out more about your favorite. Where do such scientists work? What are some projects they do?

Tools of the Trade

Marine biologists all spend many days and weeks outside their lab, visiting their area of study in person. The ocean presents a host of challenges for anyone wishing to study it. First, of course, people can't spend very much time in it unless they get help breathing. Second, the ocean is often a dark place far from the sun. How do you see when you're down there? The ocean is also not a good place for machinery or electronics. Saltwater can do great damage to just about any material. Anything electric will be especially hurt by seawater.

Those are just challenges to overcome for creative and hard-working marine biologists. Here's a look at the high-tech gear they use to visit with sea creatures of all kinds.

WORDS TO UNDERSTAND

buoyancy   the ability to float in liquid

carbon dioxide   a gas that makes up most of the air that we exhale

insulates   creates a barrier to keep out heat or cold

Breathing Underwater

For depths of up to about 125 feet (38 m), scientists can use standard scuba diving gear. Tanks worn on the back provide the air needed to breathe underwater. Depending on the temperature and depth, a diver can stay under for more than an hour at a time. Divers also wear a clear face mask that contains the breathing gear. Even if the water is warm, divers usually wear a neoprene suit. In colder waters, this suit is made of thicker material. A thin layer of water gets between the diver and the suit and is warmed by the diver's body heat. This **insulates** the diver from the cold water.

Diving creates wonderful opportunities for interacting with the sea animals being studied. Marine biologists see them in their natural surroundings, interacting with each other and their habitats. They can see many examples of some species at one time instead of just one at a time in a lab setting. Witnessing a school of fish swarming around you is very different than watching a video or holding just one fish.

Scientists head underwater with very specific goals for each dive. For instance, they might be searching a coral reef for evidence of contamination. To do that, they lay out a search grid and carefully check each block of the

Coral reefs often are filled with very colorful fish as well as the coral and rocks that they live among.

grid. They can record their observations with video and still cameras or with grease boards that let them write underwater. They also always dive in pairs or groups, which is basic diving safety.

Another kind of underwater breathing gear is called a rebreather. Instead of having tanks that use up the air as the diver breathes,

In the water, scuba divers can easily carry heavy gear, such as cameras or extra tanks.

which limits time underwater, a rebreather changes the air. That is, it takes the air the diver breathes out, scrubs out the **carbon dioxide**, and puts oxygen back into a tank for the diver to breathe again. These are very high-tech pieces of gear and not right for every diver, but they can let scientists stay down for longer periods.

Along with tanks and masks, divers usually wear fins. These wide paddles on their feet help them move more quickly and easily in the water. To control the depth at which they want to work, divers wear vests or belts that can inflate or deflate. By controlling their **buoyancy** this way, divers can hover in place while they observe their targets.

Driving Underwater

Scuba diving lets scientists work in a small area for a short time. They are also limited by how deep they can dive, which can rarely exceed 200 feet or so. To spend more time below the surface, dive deeper, and explore more area, they rely on submersibles. They are mini-submarines that usually have room for two to four scientists and drivers. Made with thick steel to handle the pressure of the deep ocean, the submersibles also have viewing ports. Using outside lights, the scientists can watch the fishy world go by as they move through the water like a metal whale.

Most submersibles have arms or baskets attached to the outside. The scientists can move the arms from inside to pick up specimens or move objects outside the sub. The baskets can be used to transport the creatures to the surface. Inside the machines, the scientists are kept warm and dry and provided with oxygen. They don't have to wear diving suits, either, and can work in comfort.

Submersibles are each used for a specific purpose. The sub called *Alvin* is run by the Woods Hole Oceanographic Institute. *Alvin* has visited some of the deepest ocean spots on the planet, helping to discover new forms of life. The sub can reach almost 15,000 feet (4,572 m) and makes as many as 200 dives a year. It goes to sea on the back of a much larger ship. The ship uses a crane to raise and lower the sub from the deck to the sea.

A Russian pair of subs called *Mir I* and *Mir II* can go below 20,000 feet (6,100 m), making them among the deepest-diving in the world. The Mirs run on batteries and can hold three people. Their ability to stay for long periods at great depths makes them excellent film-making platforms. Director James Cameron used Mir subs to help him film scenes from the motion picture *Titanic*.

The *Deepworker* sub holds just one person, but is much more maneuverable than *Alvin*. Under a large glass bubble, the driver/scientist can take measurements of the sea world outside. He or she can pick up samples or even target a laser on a sample to take readings. The size of *Deepworker* is a big advantage. By being lighter and more portable than a larger submersible, it can visit places that others can't.

Not every submersible is manned. Some are remote operated vehicles (ROVs) that shipboard drivers can steer around underwater. Most ROVs operate while tethered to a long cable that sends down power and brings back images. ROVs can operate in areas that would be dangerous for humans and can stay under for much longer periods. The National Oceanic and Atmospheric Administration (NOAA) employs ROVs such as *Hercules* and *Jason* for day-long explorations. *Hercules* can wander amid underwater thermal vents, for example, letting scientists on ships above see in real time the forces that are creating life there. ROVs also have high-definition cameras to bring back pictures and video for later study.

Underwater Lab

Dives and submersibles can take scientists under for fairly short periods. At NOAA's Aquarius Reef Base, run with Florida International University, they can be under for a week or more. Scientists in *Aquarius* live in specially pressurized buildings on the sea floor off Florida. They can venture out for dives while also doing research on what they see around them. By not having to go up and down for each dive, they can save lots of time. NOAA estimates that a 10-day *Aquarius* mission would take a scientist more than 60 days to complete the "regular" way.

Seeing Underwater

The underwater world is enormous and very, very dark. Science has solved some of the problems of "seeing" underwater with sonar. This technology acts much like a bat's echolocation. Sound waves are sent out, and their echoes are read by a machine. The machine then translates those echoes into information about how far objects are from the sonar site, whether they are moving, how big they are, and more. For marine biologists, sonar is a great way to find and track some of the kinds of animals they are studying. Schools of fish, pods of whales, or large masses of floating plants can be tracked that way. Other kinds of sonar can be used to map the ocean floor, providing a 3-D map of what is far below.

Another way that scientists see underwater is with fiber optics. Instead of large lenses on a camera body, fiber optics are very thin tubes that can transmit video pictures. The scientists can use red or green light at the end of the tube; the light does not disturb the animals but still picks up their movements.

Electronics

Electric gear and salt water do not mix well. However, science and technology have solved that problem in many cases, and electronics now play a big part in marine biology.

Following a fish or a marine mammal through hundreds or thousands of miles of ocean would be impossible for a ship, a diver, or even a sub. Electronic trackers, however, do the job. The small devices are attached to the animals without harming them. The fish or mammal is captured, measured, and checked. If it's healthy, the device is attached, and the animal returns to the water. Using satellites or radio-guidance systems, scientists can then record every move the animal makes. Sea turtles have been tracked traveling more than 3,000 miles (4,828 km), while a hammerhead shark was found to swim up and down the entire Atlantic coast of the United States.

The tracking gear can be used for animals large and small. The data from the tracker can show migration patterns, feeding habits, or depth of dives. Studying the patterns and movements can give scientists clues about the health of the species and how their lives and habitats change over time.

Along with using electronics on the animals, scientists use them in the animals' home as well. By gathering data from floating buoys, towed sensors, and trackers dropped into the sea, scientists have been able to gather enormous amounts of new information about the oceans.

Of course, all these machines must be designed to withstand the pressures and chemistry of the undersea world.

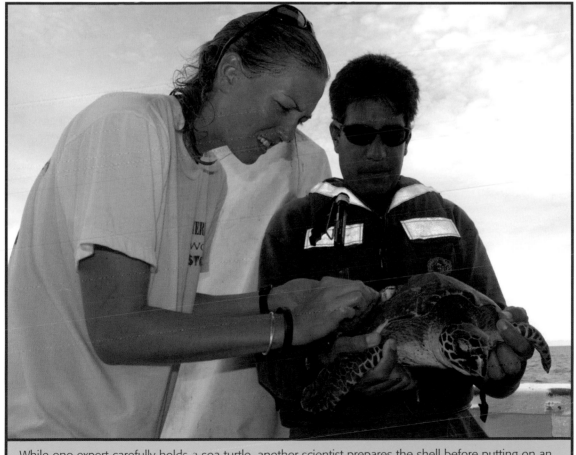

While one expert carefully holds a sea turtle, another scientist prepares the shell before putting on an electronic tracker. Satellites will help them watch as this turtle swims through the ocean.

Satellite images such as this one showing wind patterns over the islands of Hawaii have given scientists in many fields, including marine biology, new ways to gather vital information about the seas.

"We've been on the forefront of figuring out how to create new and better sensors that can work in the ocean environment," said UCSB's Carol Blanchette. "When you put a machine in the water, it soon becomes covered by algae or barnacles or other sea life. That makes it hard to measure the chemistry when the sensor is covered up. So we have to constantly try to find new sensors that work well."

Eyes in the Sky

Satellites in space play a big part in coordinating the work of all those sensors and trackers. Satellites detect and relay the signals to stations on Earth. By remaining over one place on Earth, geostationary satellites show how that place changes over time. Satellites have provided information about tides, storms, cloud patterns, and water temperatures. Satellites can even see into the ocean to map coral reefs and see how they change over time. Understanding the health of the oceans is vital to understanding the animals that live there.

Several countries have satellites that help gather this data. The United States, Japan, and the European Space Agency have all put up such craft. One of the great things about science is the worldwide co-operation. In most cases, scientists are eager to share their news and discoveries with others. Satellites help in that case, too, by beaming signals from conferences around the world so that many experts can hear the news at once.

NOAA's satellites have another big job: saving people. Because the satellites are trained on the oceans, they can be used to track ship-wrecks and people lost at sea. In 2014, for example, NOAA reported helping to save 240 people on land and sea.

 Text-Dependent Questions

1. What is the deepest dive depth by a submersible mentioned in this chapter?
2. What does sonar use to find objects underwater?
3. How far did tracking gear say a turtle traveled?

 Research Project

Read more about submersibles online. What is the greatest depth ever reached by a submersible? What is the longest time that a human has been underwater in a submersible or underwater lab such as Aquarius? What are the hazards of staying underwater too long?

Tales From the Field!

Human beings have been living with the seas and the animals in them for thousands of years. Only in the past few hundred years have experts begun studying them. Part of the problem was just reaching many parts of that vast environment. Then scientists in other fields such as engineering began to create vehicles and systems that made exploring underwater more possible then ever. Once the undersea world was open to humans, new discoveries poured out.

The work of marine biologists now spreads around the world and includes finding new animals, learning more about the animals we already know about, and finding new ways to help those animals survive.

WORDS TO UNDERSTAND

cetaceans   a class of marine mammals that includes whales

Undersea Pioneers

Until only a few decades ago, the only way to examine most marine life in its habitat was to hold your breath and take a short dive. The vast majority of the world's oceans was a dark, mysterious, airless place in which people could not go.

Submarines changed a part of that, beginning in the mid-twentieth century, although divers were still connected to the surface by long hoses that pumped air into huge, bulky helmets. Finally, in the 1940s, someone found a solution. With the invention of scuba gear that let people carry their air with them into the depths, exploration by biologists and other scientists expanded rapidly. The most famous such explorer was a French explorer named Jacques Cousteau (pictured on page 32). He was the inventor of what was first called the "aqua-lung," a tank of pressurized air that allowed breathing through a special valve. This system let Cousteau become among the first people to make extended dives. He explored shipwrecks and coral reefs, filming them for the first time with an underwater camera he also invented. His work, which later included films and TV specials, opened the undersea world to billions of people for the first time. Though not a scientist, he inspired thousands of people to become marine biologists, oceanographers, and more.

One of those early explorers was Sylvie Earle. She became a marine scientist in the 1960s and by the 1970s was diving to places few people had ever been. She later became the first woman to be the chief scientist for NOAA. Her work in submersibles and in calling attention to the health of the oceans has made her world famous. She has used her fame to get more and more people involved with helping the oceans of the world and the creatures and plants that live in them.

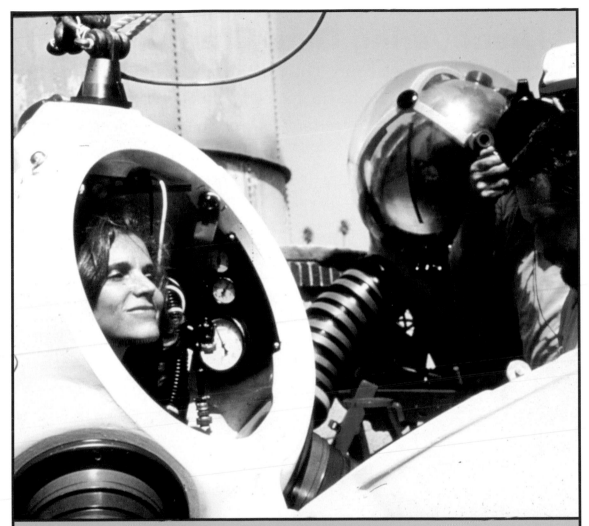

As a young scientist, Earle was fearless about finding new ways to explore the ocean up close. Her fame grew, and she used her position to spread awareness of how people are changing the seas.

"People ask: 'Why should I care about the ocean?'" she said in the movie *Bag It*, about the impact of plastic bags on the ocean. "Because the ocean is the cornerstone of Earth's life support system. It shapes climate and weather. It holds most of life on Earth. Ninety-seven percent of Earth's water is there. It's the blue heart of the planet—we should take care of our heart. It's what makes life possible for us."

Discovering New Creatures

Marine biologists are not just looking at animals that live today—they are fascinated by animals that lived millions of years ago as well. In 2014, scientists working in the deep waters of the Arctic found fossils of a clam that they had never seen before. To most people, a clam is a clam. To experts, however, there can be many small, but important, differences.

Brian Edwards was the scientist who dug up the fossils while doing a mapping study with experts from the United States and Canada.

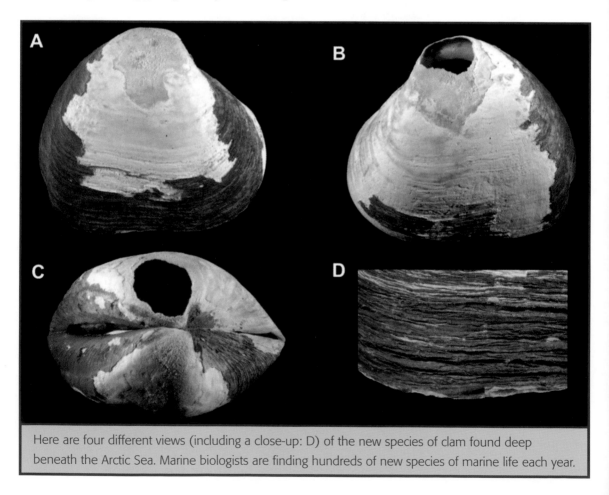

Here are four different views (including a close-up: D) of the new species of clam found deep beneath the Arctic Sea. Marine biologists are finding hundreds of new species of marine life each year.

As he and others sorted through their findings back at their lab, they found one clam fossil they did not recognize. Might this be something new?

They called in a clam expert named Paul Valentich-Scott. Working like a detective, Valentich-Scott scoured the scientific records and contacted museums around the world. After he and others looked carefully, they realized they might have something never before discovered: a new species of clam.

They wrote up their findings, and when they were published, marine history had a new story to talk about: the debut of *Wallerconcha sarea*, a 1.8-million-year-old clam. Part of the name came from Sara, the daughter of one of the crew that discovered the animal. Scientists who discover new species get to pick the name!

Naming Animals

All animals have a scientific name that identifies them. No matter what language an expert speaks, he or she will know an animal by that Latin name. The process of naming animals is called "taxonomy." The classification of animals in that way was created in the 1700s by a Swedish scientist named Carl Linneaus. The two parts of each name are the genus (JEEN-us) and the species (SPEE-shees). For example, a humpback whale is *Megaptera novaeangliae*. What the whale calls itself, of course, remains a mystery.

"It is always exciting when you are the first person to be looking at a new creature," said Valentich-Scott.

Finding new types of marine creatures sometimes means looking right under your nose. Scientists knew that there were at least three types of humpback dolphins, including one that lived in the waters off Australia. However, as they looked at records dating back centuries and compared them to new scientific studies, including DNA and similar tools, they found something they didn't expect.

"We've finally managed to settle many long-standing questions about humpback dolphins—particularly how many species actually exist—using a huge body of data collected over two centuries and analyzed with the latest scientific tools," said Dr. Thomas Jefferson, the biologist who led the study.

In 2014, his team announced it had found that the Australian humpback dolphin, which they named *Sousa sahulensis*, was different enough to be its own species. The Australian now joins humpbacks from the Indian Ocean, Atlantic Ocean, and Pacific Ocean as part of this four-species genus.

Up to one million different species of animals live in the oceans. Scientists think as many as 500,000 more have yet to be found and named. So that's two down and 499,998 to go!

Another Reason to Love Whales

As the story at the beginning of this book showed, whales need our help sometimes. However, it turns out they are also providing a lot of help themselves. Scientists studying whales put out a report that showed that whales are doing much more good than just giving whale-watching boats something to look at.

Biologist Joe Roman from the University of Vermont led a team that looked at the impact of whales on ocean- and marine-life health in general. What they found is actually kind of gross, but truly helpful.

"As humpbacks, gray whales, sperm whales, and other **cetaceans** recover from centuries of overhunting, we are beginning to see that they also play an important role in the ocean," Roman said. "Among their many ecological roles, whales recycle nutrients and enhance primary productivity in areas where they feed."

Whales recycle by eating tons of food every day, then rising to near the surface to poop. Their discharge in the water or drifting to the bottom provides food for plankton and other tiny creatures living throughout the sea. Then the whales dive back to eat again. At the end of their lives, whales provide recycling again. When they die, most of

Whales have proven to be a big part of the ocean food chain. Their waste products help create an environment for small animals to live in, while their remains provide food for fish and crabs.

Just beyond this boat filled with scientists is a floating whale carcass. The experts are taking samples and photos before the animal sinks.

their bodies sink to the bottom, an action called a "whale fall." Once there, they become a huge food source for thousands of fish, crabs, and other animals.

"Dozens, possibly hundreds, of species depend on these whale falls in the deep sea," Roman noted.

So marine biologists have found that whales are giving back in more ways than one, adding more pressure on humans to take care of them around the world.

Are Sea Stars in Trouble?

Sea stars are a type of marine animal called an echinoderm. Scientists along the California coast noticed that the numbers of sea stars were decreasing. Many of those that remained seemed very sick with a disease that slowly broke apart their bodies.

"We've had epidemics [of disease] before, but never anything like this," UCLA's Richard Ambrose told the *Los Angeles Times*. "We saw some sea stars with lesions [sores] at some sites, and a week later, all the sea stars were gone."

Sea stars (not starfish!) are living creatures, part of a class called echinoderms (ee-KYE-noh-dermz). If they lose one of their limbs, they often can grow a new one.

Sea-Star Sight

A pair of scientists had their eye on eyes—sea-star eyes, to be exact. Marine biologists knew sea stars have eyes. The eyes are tiny spots located on the ends of the animal's arms. Until Anders Garm of Denmark and Dan-Eric Nilsson of Sweden did some experiments, we didn't know how those eyes worked. First, the sea-star experts looked at the eye parts under a very large microscope. After understanding the structure of the eye, they did an experiment to see how well sea stars could find their way back to a rock home using only their eyesight. The investigation continues, but the breakthrough was knowing just how sharp those sea-star eyes can be.

To find the cause of the illness, biologists put on their wading boots and hit the beach. They gathered dead, sick, and healthy animals from many places.

In their labs, they tested and tested. For a while, they were stumped. After looking at several possibilities, they zeroed in their search on a virus.

Knowing what was wrong, however, did not give them answers on how to help. Sometimes scientists can only watch and wait. A few months after first spotting the illness, scientists saw baby starfish coming back in record numbers.

"We saw more juveniles than we had in the past fifteen years," said Peter Raimondi, a scientist at the University of California at Santa Cruz.

Will the illness come back? Marine biologists up and down the coast will be watching carefully.

Whales, sea stars, clams—plus thousands of species of fish of every size, shape and color—they are the study subjects of marine biologists. Using science, creativity, and some high-tech gear, they continue to explore the oceans of the world. With 70 percent of the world to explore, they have only just begun to find out all they can about the amazing life forms that lives beneath the waves.

 # Text-Dependent Questions

1. What was Jacques Cousteau's big invention?
2. What kind of animal did Brian Edwards find?
3. How do whales help us and the ocean?

 # Research Project

Do you have a favorite sea animal? Do some online research to find a study that is looking at that animal. Someone somewhere is studying just about every animal in the ocean, so dig around until you find your favorite. What did scientists find out? Where are they working? How are they doing experiments?

Good News for Turtles

Sea turtles are some of the most traveled animals on the planet. They can swim for thousands of miles, usually in a big circle to and from their beach nesting grounds. However, those long trips put them in contact with many dangers. They are caught up in fishing nets, hunted for food, hit by ships, and hurt by eating plastic thrown in the ocean. So it was good news when a study in Nicaragua saw a big increase in the count of hawksbill turtles there, which rose 200 percent in the first part of the 2000s. A big reason was the help that people gave the animals' eggs. Sea turtles lay their eggs in pits on a beach. Other animals, even pet dogs, can dig those eggs up and eat them. Locals in Nicaragua began guarding the nest sites. This helped more baby turtles be born, increasing the population. Similar turtle-guarding programs are at work in Florida, the Carolinas, Central America, and the Caribbean.

Another turtle rescue took place in Massachusetts. A species called the Kemp's ridley sea turtle likes to eat in Cape Cod Bay. In some years, the water gets too cold too fast, and they can be trapped. Rescuers pluck them out and transport them to warmer waters in the South. In 2014, a record number had to be rescued and flown by Coast Guard planes to their new homes.

Cars Made From Limpets?

A limpet is a shellfish, somewhat like an underwater snail. The tiny animals live inside a hard outer shell. Scientists in England found that the material the shell is made of might have other uses. The material, called goethite, is arranged at the atomic level in a way scientists haven't seen before. Dr. Asa Barber of the University of Portsmouth thinks it might be the strongest natural material in the world. "Generally, a big structure has lots of flaws and can break more easily than a smaller structure, which has fewer flaws and is stronger," he said. "The problem is that most structures have to be fairly big so they're weaker than we would like. Limpet teeth break this rule as their strength is the same no matter what the size." Barber suggests that further study might show the structure could make cars, boats, and planes lighter and stronger.

Protecting Seals

NOAA is one of many groups working with marine biologists to identify animals in trouble. In the waters off Alaska, NOAA is tracking populations of ringed seals. They are trying to get the U.S. government to create areas in which the seals can be protected. This is just one of many examples where national and local governments are making laws to protect sea animals. The 1972 Marine Mammal Protection Act covers all of America's coastal waters. The act makes it illegal, in most cases, to capture or kill animals such as dolphins, seals, or sea lions. Thanks to this and other laws, many species of marine mammals have come back from the edge of extinction.

Find Out More

Books

Castro, Peter, and Michael Huber. *Marine Biology*. New York: McGraw-Hill Science/Engineering/Math, 2012.

Karleskint, George. *Introduction to Marine Biology*. Boston: Cengage Learning, 2012.

McCalman, Iain. *The Reef: A Passionate History: The Great Barrier Reef From Captain Cook to Climate Change*. New York: Scientific American/Farrar, Straus and Giroux, 2015.

Middleton, Susan. *Spineless*. New York: Harry N. Abrams, 2014.
Note: An award-winning photo book featuring marine invertebrates (animals without backbones, such as octopuses, squid, and snails).

Web Sites

www.education.noaa.gov
Visit this site to look for ways you can work with NOAA in various marine biology internships.

marinebio.org
The MarineBio Conservation Society has a large Web site with information about careers, marine science news, and special sections on global warming, fisheries, pollution, and more.

www.marinecareers.net
Look into the many fields of marine biology on this site from the famous Woods Hole Oceanographic Institute.

Series Glossary of Key Terms

airlock a room on a space station from which astronauts can move from inside to outside the station and back

anatomy a branch of knowledge that deals with the structure of organisms

bionic to be assisted by mechanical movements

carbon dioxide a gas that is in the air that we breathe out

classified kept secret from all but a few people in a government or an organization

deforestation the destruction of forest or woodland

diagnose to recognize by signs and symptoms

discipline in science, this means a particular field of study

elite the part or group having the highest quality or importance

genes information stored in cells that determine a person's physical characteristics

geostationary remaining in the same place above the Earth during an orbit

innovative groundbreaking, original

inquisitiveness an ability to be curious, to continue asking questions to learn more

internships jobs often done for free by people in the early stages of study for a career

marine having to do with the ocean

meteorologist a scientist who forecasts weather and weather patterns

physicist a scientist who studies physics, which examines how matter and energy move and relate

primate a type of four-limbed mammal with a developed brain; includes humans, apes, and monkeys

traits a particular quality or personality belonging to a person

Index

Photo Credits

About the Author

K.C. Kelley has written dozens of nonfiction books for young readers on topics as wide as space, animals, nature, robots, baseball, history, careers, and, of course, marine biologists.